Tune Your Guitar

by Matt Scharfglass

A fun and easy guide to tuning your guitar. Much more than just a tuning guide, this handy little book and CD package offers tuning demonstrations, musical examples of different tunings, and much more.

Cover photography by Randall Wallace and William Draffen
Project editor: Ed Lozano
Interior design and layout: Len Vogler
Interior photography: Sandra Dubrov and Randall Wallace

This book Copyright © 2000 by Amsco Publications,
A Division of Music Sales Corporation, New York

All rights reserved. No part of this book may be reproduced in any form or by any electronic or mechanical means, including information storage and retrieval systems, without permission in writing from the publisher.

Order No. AM 961477
US International Standard Book Number: 0.8256.1768.5
UK International Standard Book Number: 0.7119.7894.8

Exclusive Distributors:
Music Sales Corporation
257 Park Avenue South, New York, NY 10010 USA
Music Sales Limited
8/9 Frith Street, London W1D 3JB England
Music Sales Pty. Limited
120 Rothschild Street, Rosebery, Sydney, NSW 2018, Australia

Printed in the United States of America by
Vicks Lithograph and Printing Corporation

Amsco Publications
New York/London/Paris/Sydney/Tokyo/Copenhagen/Madrid

Contents

Introduction 3
Part 1: Tuning Methods 5
   A. Finding That First Pitch 5
   B. Coarse Tuning: Tuning by 5th Frets 6
   C. Fine Tuning: Tuning by Harmonics 8
   D. Fine-Fine Tuning 10
   E. Making Sure You're in Tune 11
   F. Open-Mic Night at the Club… revisited 11
Part 2: Why Guitars Go Out of Tune 13
   A. Hard Strumming 13
   B. Warping or Bowing of the Neck 13
   C. Troubleshooting a Warped Neck 14
   D. Rough Handling 14
   E. Intonation 15
   F. Strings 16
   G. When Disaster Strikes! 17
Part 3: Altered Tunings 19
   A. Standard Tuning Down One Half-Step
      (low to high: E♭ A♭ D♭ G♭ B♭ E♭) 19
   B. Drop D Tuning (low to high: D A D G B E) 20
   C. Open D Tuning (low to high: D A D F♯ A D) 21
   D. Open G Tuning (low to high: D G D G B D) 24
Appendix: Changing Your Strings 26
   A. Steel-String Acoustic 27
   B. Nylon-String Acoustic 28
   C. Electric, Front or Bridge-Loading, Non-Tremolo 29
   D. Electric, Rear-Loading with Standard, Non-Locking Tremolo 30
   E. Bass 30
Further Reading 31
About the Author 32

CD Track List

1. Introduction
2. E Reference Pitch
3. A Reference Pitch
4. D Reference Pitch
5. G Reference Pitch
6. B Reference Pitch
7. High E Reference Pitch
8. Tuning by 5th Frets
9. Tuning by Harmonics
10. Tuning to Chords
11. Introduction to Altered Tunings
12. Down One Half-Step Tuning (Reference Pitches)
13. Down One Half-Step Tuning – Musical Example
14. Drop D Tuning (Reference Pitches)
15. Drop D Tuning – Musical Example
16. Open D Tuning (Reference Pitches)
17. Open D Tuning – Musical Example
18. Open G Tuning (Reference Pitches)
19. Open G Tuning – Musical Example
20. Troubleshooting Tuning Problems

Introduction

Buy this tuner! It fits in your guitar case, has a direct input so you can plug your instrument straight into it, and it has this special fancy doodad you can press for tuning low frequency instruments such as bass!

No, wait… buy this tuner! It's a really expensive rack mount type, which means it must be the kind that only the pros use. After all, it'll tell you the correct pitch to the cent! And let's not forget all those cool lights and buttons that make it look like the perfect compliment to any guitar rack system. Accessorize, baby!

All kidding aside… what the big instrument manufacturers don't want you to remember is that for centuries before us, people used a much cheaper, much more portable, and in some cases even more reliable method of tuning instruments: their ears.

That's right, folks. Ears. Most of us have 'em, and we usually bring them wherever we go. Of course, some of us are more attuned to pitch problems than others; but even the must unmusical, tone-deaf person can tell when someone is singing or playing out of tune. Maybe they can't articulate exactly what it is that's wrong, but they can at least tell you if it sounds bad.

There are many reasons why tuners aren't necessarily your friend. Here are just a couple:

- It's open-mic night at your local club. You meticulously fine tune your guitar at home with your tuner, carefully place the instrument in its gig bag so as not to disturb the tuning pegs, and leave for the gig. You walk twenty minutes to the club in the thick, humid air (did I mention that it's July and you're in New York?). You show up, pull out your instrument and wait for the house band to call you up. At which point you get on stage, plug in, and after only a few seconds of playing you find that you are out of tune. Performing out of tune is unprofessional, but even worse is stopping to retune, so you sheepishly continue your performance.

- It's open-mic night at your local club. You meticulously fine tune your guitar with your tuner at the club, because you know what humidity does to instruments. The house band is already playing and there's a lot of crowd noise, but luckily you have that direct input on your tuner. So, you take your tuner's word for it that everything's okay, even though you haven't heard it for yourself. The house band calls you up on stage, you plug in, the piano player starts the intro to the song and… uh oh, you're out of tune.

How did this happen? Looks like the rest of the band tuned up to the piano, obviously because even if the piano itself is not in tune, it's just much easier to go with it then retune it!

To be fair, an electronic tuner definitely has its place in two kinds of situations. Guitar builders and repair personnel use them when testing neck set-ups to ensure that an instrument is in tune with itself. Tuners are also useful when recording, although this may not apply to situations where keyboards are involved, for two reasons:

- If it's a piano, you can forget about tuning it to the proper tuner pitch. Tuning a piano is a specialized and time-consuming task best left to professionals.

- I recently recorded a CD. I used the same tuner for all basses and guitars. Upon listening back, I felt the music needed another texture, so I decided to add a little synth. Well, synths are digital, so their pitches must always be perfect, right? Wrong! Sometimes tuners or electronic instruments are calibrated to different tones; consequently, an A440 on a keyboard may not be the same as the A440 on a tuner. So, I had no choice but to use my ears to tune the synth to the rest of the music.

The "open-mic night" scenarios above illustrate a problem that is all too common these days: musicians who are lost without their tuners. There is nothing more annoying to a music fan than a band that can't play in tune, or one that has to stop after every song and plug into their tuners *right there on stage.*

Your electronic tuner is fine if you remember that it's a tool, not a *crutch*. In this book, along with the accompanying CD, we will learn how to rely less on tuners by helping you develop the skills necessary to gain confidence in what should be your most valuable assets as a music maker: your own ears.

Part 1: Tuning Methods

A. Finding That First Pitch

If you're going to tune without the aid of a tuner, and you don't have perfect pitch, then you'll need a reliable starting point.

To begin, we'll use the reference pitches provided on the accompanying audio recording. Track 2 is a low E note. Play the track and pluck your low E string to hear how they relate to each other. Listen carefully to see if your low E is higher or lower than the reference pitch on the CD, then slowly tune the string accordingly.

When you've tuned up your low E, take a minute to do the same for the other five strings. (CD Tracks 3-7)

Finished? Good! Now detune all of your strings because we're going to try something different.

Tuning up to a given reference pitch is relatively easy; but what do you do if that pitch is not readily available?

Tune to a piano.

This is especially effective if you're at a gig where the band has a keyboard player. If he or she is using a synthesizer or electric keyboard instead of a real piano then tune to that because, as you probably know, it's much more difficult to tune a synthesizer than it is for everyone to just tune to the synth instead.

If you're on a gig, this is fine. But what if you're at home and you don't own a piano?

Tune to your favorite song.

That's right, grab a CD, pop it in the player and tune to it as you play along. This method is foolproof as long as: (a) you know the song, and (b) it's not performed by a band that always plays everything tuned down one half-step. Artists such as Metallica, Extreme, Jimi Hendrix, and David Lee Roth-era Van Halen would customarily drop the pitches of their instruments by one half-step to make it easier for their vocalists to hit the higher notes. *(See the section on "Standard Tuning One Half-Step Down" in Part 3.)*

The average music listener or beginning musician won't have any way of knowing which bands do this and which bands don't, so you'll have to do some homework. Pick a song, track down a guitar transcription (music stores are full of these, so it shouldn't be too difficult), and find out what key the song is in. Examples:

"Plush" by Stone Temple Pilots – key of G
"What's this Life For" by Creed – key of G
"What I Got" by Sublime – key of D
"No Shelter" by Rage Against the Machine – key of Dm
"Falls Apart" by Sugar Ray – key of E
"Iron Man" by Black Sabbath – key of Em
"Dirty Deeds Done Dirt Cheap" by AC/DC – key of E
"Faith" by Limp Bizkit – key of B
"Jeremy" by Pearl Jam – keys of A and A minor (depends on which section of the song!)
"Got the Life" by Korn – Am

Notice that these songs are in open keys, or keys whose primary chords use open strings. For example, since you now know that "Jeremy" is in the key of A, you can tune your A string to that song. Likewise, you can tune your high and low E strings to "Falls Apart," "Iron Man," or just about any AC/DC song. The key here is that when you hum a song to yourself in your head, you'll probably hear it in its correct pitch, and that should give you a starting point.

When I was thirteen and still coming up as a musician, my starting point was "Beat It" by Michael Jackson, because I knew that the very first note of the song, played on a synthesizer, was a G. Hey! Don't laugh! I only liked that song because Eddie Van Halen played a really cool solo on it!

It's important to use whichever song you pick as a starting point consistently. Even if you hate the song a year from now, you'll at least have it burned into your memory so you'll always have that reference pitch.

B. Coarse Tuning: Tuning by 5th Frets

Now that you have that first pitch, you can tune the rest of the instrument.

Let's say you tuned to an E. That means your lowest (or sixth) string is now at its proper pitch, so we can move on to the next lowest string, the A or fifth string.

Put your finger on the 5th fret of the low E (or sixth) string, and play the note. Hold the note for a few seconds; then play the open A (or fifth) string. The pitch of the open A should be the same as that of the fretted note. If the open A string sounds a little higher, then you need to loosen it by tuning it *down*. Conversely, if it's too low, you need to tighten it by tuning it up. Basically, we're doing exactly what we did at the beginning of the chapter when you tuned to the reference pitch on the CD, only now you're providing your own reference pitch, which is the note on the 5th fret of the low E string!

A little tuning trick: As you tune the A string against the note being played on the 5th fret of the E string, you'll probably notice a pulsing between the notes. This is what happens when two notes are close together in pitch but slightly out of tune. As you tune the A string closer to its correct pitch, you'll hear the pulsing become slower. When it's nonexistent, you'll know that the string is in tune. This phenomenon is covered on Track 8 of the CD.

After you match these two pitches, do the same for the D (or fourth) string. Put your finger on the 5th fret of the A string and play the note; then pluck the open D string. If the open D string doesn't match the fretted A string, tune it accordingly; then tune the G (or third) string in the same manner.

For the B (or second) string, we'll alter this technique a bit by fretting the G string on the 4th fret instead of the 5th. Like before, the open B string should produce the same pitch as the fretted note.

Now fret the B string at the 5th fret to tune the high E (or first) string.

When you think you've gotten the high E in tune, test it by playing the low and high Es together.

Here's a chart to sum this technique up.

> 5th fret of the low E (or sixth) string =
> open A (or fifth) string
>
> 5th fret of the A (or fifth) string =
> open D (or fourth) string
>
> 5th fret of the D (or fourth) string =
> open G (or third) string
>
> 4th fret of the G (or third) string =
> open B (or second) string
>
> 5th fret of the B (or second) string =
> open high E (or first) string

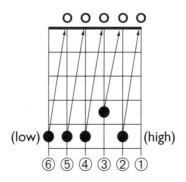

C. Fine Tuning: Tuning by Harmonics

You've gotten all the strings more or less in tune... now we'll get them perfectly in tune.

A *harmonic* is a bell-like tone produced by lightly touching a string directly over the fret while plucking it. The key is to lightly touch the string without pressing it down. Each string has an infinite amount of harmonic locations; some are inaudible while others are used frequently for effect. The introductions to Rush's "Red Barchetta" and Yes' "Roundabout" come to mind.

We will deal with three main harmonic locations. These harmonics are located at the 5th, 7th, and 12th frets.

Touch the high E string directly over the 12th fret, but don't press down.

Now pluck the string and quickly take your fretting finger off of it. If you did it correctly you'll hear an E which sounds one octave above the open E string.

Now, let's try the 7th fret harmonic. Touch the A string directly over the 7th fret, and again, don't press down. When you pluck the string, you'll hear an E again, only it will sound two octaves higher than the open low E string.

Finally, the 5th fret harmonic. Touch the low E string directly over the 5th fret, and pluck the string. You'll notice that the pitch produced is the same as the pitch you just produced at the 7th fret harmonic on the A string.

The point of all this? With the exception of the B string, *the harmonic produced at the 5th fret of a string will sound like the harmonic produced at the 7th fret of the following string.*

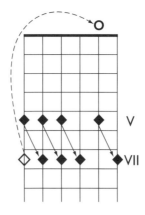

We will take advantage of this wonderful principle of sound physics by applying it to a tuning technique known as *tuning by harmonics*.

Since we know that your low E string is in tune, we'll begin by tuning the A string to it. Using the harmonic at the 5th fret of the E string as your reference pitch, play the harmonic at the 7th fret of the A string against it. Like before, if you hear that the pitches don't match, or you hear a pulsing between the two notes, then the A string is out of tune and will need to be adjusted accordingly. Listen to Track 9 on the CD for a demonstration of this technique.

When you are finished with the A string, do the same for the D and G strings.

The B string now complicates everything again because it's tuned to a different interval than the rest of the strings. E, A, D, and G are all a perfect fourth apart from each other, but the B string, troublemaker that it is, is a major third from the G string. The high E is a perfect fourth from the B. Don't worry, we won't get into a theory discussion here; this is just information provided to help you understand why the B string has to be tuned differently.

With that in mind, let's tune up the B string. Touch the harmonic on low E at the 7th fret and tune the open B string accordingly.

Now resume the 5th fret/7th fret harmonics tuning method to tune the high E to the B.

TIP: If you're having a particularly hard time tuning one string to another (to the point where your ears are becoming fatigued), try deliberately tuning the errant string way too low in relation to the "good" string. Now take a deep breath, fight the urge to smash your instrument, and slowly start tuning the "bad" string up to pitch. As the "out-of-tune" pulsings become slower, you'll hear that the strings are getting closer to being in tune. This tip should help you whether you are coarse tuning or fine tuning.

Here's another chart to sum up the tuning-by-harmonics method.

harmonic at the 5th fret of the low E (or sixth) string = harmonic at the 7th fret of the A (or fifth) string

harmonic at the 5th fret of the A (or fifth) string = harmonic at the 7th fret of the D (or fourth) string

harmonic at the 5th fret of the D (or fourth) string = harmonic at the 7th fret of the G (or third) string

harmonic at the 7th fret of the low E (or sixth) string = the B (or second) string open

harmonic at the 5th fret of the B (or second) string = harmonic at the 7th fret of the high E (or first) string

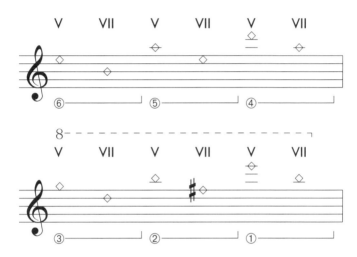

D. Fine-Fine Tuning

Some of you who own guitars which have fine tuners located on the bridge or tremolo system may have noticed that I haven't mentioned them yet. For the uninitiated, here's what fine tuners look like:

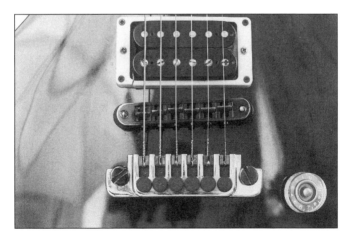

Fine tuners are great, but only if you have them. Most basses and certainly all acoustic guitars do not have them, so for this reason I have excluded them. It's also good to think of them as a last resort. If you

rely on them too much you'll never know how to tune your acoustic guitar, your bass, or that cool electric you borrowed from your friend because yours broke when your brother knocked it off the guitar stand while playing basketball in the basement.

E. Making Sure You're in Tune

Is it soup yet? Not quite. Before launching into those hair-raising, awe-inspiring guitar histrionics you might want to play a few open fifth chords, otherwise known as power chords.

They're called *open fifth chords* because they use open strings. Some chords I find useful for tuning are G5, D5, and A5.

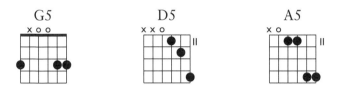

Strum each chord and then pluck each note individually while listening for clunkers. Then do whatever tweaking is necessary. This tuning technique is demonstrated on Track 10 of the CD.

F. Open-Mic Night at the Club... revisited

OK. You're at that club again, and this time you're not gonna be out of tune!

Get there early.

This way, if there's a piano, you can tune up to it and not have to worry about it later.

Well, I can't get there early, but I can get there during the first couple of songs.

All right... then tune your instrument up beforehand as best as you can, and double-check it when you get to the club. How are you supposed to do that with all that music and crowd noise and without a tuner? We'll get to that in a minute.

AHHHH! I hit a bunch of traffic on the way, I just got here, and I only have a minute to tune up!

Fahgeddaboutit! Find the bathroom. It's never good to play a gig with a full bladder.

Actually, the real reason you need the bathroom is because it: (a) is relatively quiet and (b) has walls. Well, of course it has walls, but why is this important?

Walls resonate when something vibrates against them. If you bring your guitar or bass into the bathroom and touch the headstock to the wall, any note you play will vibrate through the wall (or stall) and produce a weak but audible pitch. Poof... instant amplifier! Try it on any wall in your house.

Here's what to do:
- Once you've located the bathroom in a club, press the headstock of your guitar or bass to the wall. Enter one of the stalls if you have to (just look underneath first to make sure it isn't occupied) and touch the wall of the stall.

- *Now remember that starting pitch we talked about earlier.* In your case, it's from Billy Ray Cyrus' "Achy Breaky Heart" (key of A). Find the first chord of the song in your head, hum it to yourself out loud if you need to, and tune up that A string!

- *Bass players:* You may have trouble hearing such a low pitch at such a weak volume; to get around this, pluck the 12th fret harmonic instead and tune to that pitch.

- After you've gotten it in tune, you can tune the rest of the instrument to the A string.

The good news is that there are other tricks you can employ to tune up at the club. Just use your head. Literally...

The head against the table trick: This utilizes the principle described a minute ago where we produced a somewhat audible pitch by putting the headstock of the guitar against a wall (or bathroom stall). This time, we're merely replacing the wall with an ordinary bar table. Simply sit down, relax, and hold the instrument under the table; then put the headstock against the underside of the table and press your ear to the table surface as you play whatever string you're tuning.

The head against the guitar trick: Ain't got a table or wall? Why not put your head (or more accurately, your ear) against the guitar itself?!

If you really want to show off, try the head-against-the-guitar-in-the-bathroom-without-using-a-wall trick! But seriously, folks, use the bathroom trick or either of the "head against" tricks (or any combination thereof)... and you'll be able to approach the stage with a reasonable degree of confidence.

Please keep in mind that with experience, you will become very quick at dealing with tuning problems. Stay tuned for Part 2 where we discuss these problems, and deal with what to do *When Disaster Strikes!*

Part 2: Why Guitars Go Out of Tune

Many, many factors contribute to tuning problems. Here we will deal with the most common of these.

A. Hard Strumming

Aggressive playing, especially on lighter strings, will cause strings to detune slightly over the course of a few songs. This is not to say you should always play timidly—by all means, bash to your heart's delight—just remember to quickly check your tuning every couple of songs if things do start to sound funny.

B. Warping or Bowing of the Neck

Weather

Your guitar's neck, being made of wood or some kind of wood compound, is susceptible to all sorts of detuning nasties. As mentioned in the introduction, something as mundane as the weather can wreak havoc on your instrument's neck.

How? Paper is made from wood. Paper bends or curls when you drip water on it or expose it to a humid environment. In the same way, a guitar neck will begin to curl after prolonged exposure to humidity. It's certainly not fatal, but it may require you to check your tuning more often than you normally would. Just something to keep in mind.

Prolonged String Tension

A major suggestion: remember to completely slacken all of your guitar strings if you're not going to be using the instrument for a while. Constant tension on a guitar neck which is just sitting in a corner unused will cause the neck to curl forward, causing the strings and neck to resemble a crossbow. This process will occur even faster if a major seasonal change is underway.

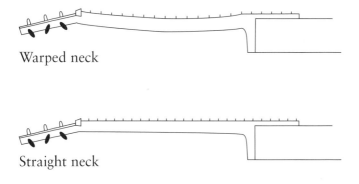

Warped neck

Straight neck

I learned this point the hard way a few years ago. I have a mandolin—a beautiful sounding instrument. I'd dabble with it in little creative bursts, put it away for a few months, then come back to it, and so on. Well, about three years went by between creative bursts on this particular occasion and I forgot to completely detune the strings. These strings consistently applied their fully-tuned tension to the neck and body of this fragile instrument for a period of thirty-six months without a minute of relief. When I finally got the urge to play the mandolin I noticed that the neck was severely warped and the body had begun to crack. Two of the strings actually broke from all the pressure. A couple of hundred bucks later everything was okay, but the ending might not have been so happy had I let any more time go by.

C. Troubleshooting a Warped Neck

How do you know if your guitar's neck is warped? Guitar builders and technicians employ a technique known as *sighting down a neck* (or fretboard). Stand your guitar on the floor or on a table and position it in such a way that the bridge is aligned with the nut. Now look down the length of the fretboard from the top of the instrument toward the bridge and check to see if the frets appear to be absolutely parallel to each other. If they are not, then your guitar's neck is warped. You can try adjusting your guitar's truss rod to correct this (you'll probably need an Allen wrench), but you might be better off bringing it to a guitar shop for adjustment especially if you're unsure of what you're doing. This kind of repair is often quick and inexpensive.

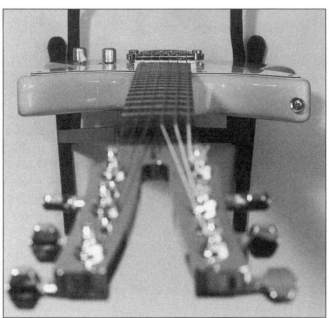

D. Rough Handling

Let's say you just spent a good deal of effort tuning up your instrument, and you have a few minutes before the show starts, so you put the guitar on its stand while you go greet your hordes of adoring fans.

Now the show is about to start, so you go backstage, grab the guitar by the middle of the neck and put it on in a hurry. Stop! Grabbing the neck will move it where it meets the body by as much as a millimeter or two. This may not sound like a big deal, but your strings will beg to differ. Lifting the guitar carefully by the area of the neck where it meets the body, or even by the body itself, is probably the best way to minimize neck movement.

As a guitar transcriber, I often have to play parts I've just written to make sure they're correct. Consequently, I keep a cheap, horrible-sounding old electric by my side because I know that the neck will have to take the abuse of being picked up and put down about 150 times a day. I try not to use my "good" guitar for transcribing.

E. Intonation

Has this ever happened to you? You get all your strings perfectly in tune, you play for a few seconds, and you hear a chord that sounds out of tune, so you stop to retune, only to find that your open strings are in tune? This is most likely an *intonation* problem.

When a guitar is intonated, every note, no matter where it's located on the fretboard, is perfectly in tune. For example, if you play a C on the 1st fret of the B string, it should produce exactly the same pitch as a C on the 5th fret of the G string, a C on the 10th fret of the D string, or a C on the 15th fret of the A string, *etc.*

Troubleshooting this is simple. Be sure your guitar is tuned to pitch, and play the harmonic at the 12th fret of any string; then fret the same string at the 12th fret. If the fretted note doesn't match the harmonic, then you have an intonation problem. Listen to Track 20 on the CD for a demonstration of this troubleshooting technique.

Improper intonation can be corrected by adjusting the length of the string. If you play electric guitar or bass, this is accomplished by tightening or loosening the string's intonation screw, which is located at the bridge. (Acoustic guitarists: sorry...in your case you'll have to bring it to the shop!)

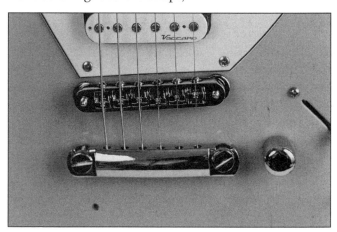

If the fretted 12th fret note is sharp in relation to the harmonic, then you'll need to tighten the intonation screw. Conversely, if the fretted 12th fret note is flat in relation to the harmonic, then you'll need to loosen the intonation screw. Remember to be sure that your guitar is perfectly tuned up to pitch while making these adjustments.

In the introduction to this book I mentioned that tuners are used by guitar repair personnel to help ensure that an instrument is in tune with itself. Checking your guitar's intonation is an example of such an occasion where you may find a tuner helpful.

F. Strings

There are three main issues to deal with here: new strings, old strings, and string breakage.

New Strings

New strings need time to settle on an instrument. This applies to both guitar and bass, but more so for guitar, as bass strings are much heavier and consequently not as prone to movement or slippage.

When you put fresh strings on a guitar and tune it up to pitch, the strings will have a tendency to slip out of tune for a few hours until they settle. In an ideal situation, it's a good rule of thumb to give new strings about a day to settle before an important gig or recording. However, strings break during recording sessions and gigs and must be replaced as soon as possible, so there are ways to get around this.

The best way is to literally yank the new strings once you've tuned them up to pitch. Just grab the string at around the 12th fret, and pull it to either side of the fretboard as far as you can a few times (without breaking it, of course!). This will completely detune the string, and you'll have to tune it up again but it also forces the string to settle faster.

Keep doing this until the string only goes slightly out of tune when you pull on it; at this point, it's probably "safe."

Old Strings

Old, or aged, strings are great because they've settled and require infrequent retuning; however, they eventually start going out of tune all the time. Sure, you can get them up to pitch, but they'll go out as soon as you bend a note or strum hard. I don't believe they need to be changed according to some kind of schedule, or even if they've begun to rust (you actually need slightly cruddy strings to get certain cool guitar sounds). But if it's taking you longer to tune than usual, ask yourself when was the last time you changed strings, and therein may lie the problem.

String Breakage

Many guitars, especially those with tremolo systems, are vulnerable to massive tuning problems if a string breaks. What happens is that when the strings are put on and tuned to their proper pitches, the neck settles into a position that supports the string tension. (Assuming you have a decent instrument, the tension is more or less balanced along the neck.) When a string breaks, that component of tension which contributes to the balance is suddenly gone, causing the overall balance to fall apart, thereby causing the other strings to go out of tune (they'll go sharp when this happens). This is where your newly-developed-super-string-tuning-powers are needed!

I actually saw a major label band (I won't name names) crumble during a TV performance when their lead guitarist busted a string early in the song. Not only could she not fake her way through the rest of the song, but her guitar went terribly out of tune as a result. And, like so many other musicians dependent on electronic tuners, she couldn't quickly retune during the song. Which brings us to....

G. When Disaster Strikes!

So, what do you do in this situation?
- Stay calm and *keep playing*. If you are horribly out of tune, then play softly, but keep playing. All you can do now is minimize the damage, and how you handle yourself will show others how professional you are.

- Depending on which string is broken, you may have to find other locations on the fretboard with which to play your part; I once had to play an entire song on the A string of an upright bass because I broke the D string. So it's a good idea to know more than one way to play a D chord! Also, don't be afraid to alter or "fake" the part as needed.

- Try to get the broken string out of your way. What I do in this kind of situation is try to "tap out" the part with my fretting hand while using my picking hand to move the broken string. Hopefully the string won't be in your way to begin with, so you can immediately focus on retuning.

- Everyone in the band will still be playing. While continuing on as best as you can, wait for a part that has open chords, such as a G, D, A, or E. When such a part comes up, take advantage of the opportunity of not having to use your fretting hand and try to tune to that open chord. Even if you can only get your hand free for a second, it's better than nothing. If you're playing a song that's in a key which doesn't contain open chords (such as the keys of A♭ or E♭) then keep fretting the part and reach over to the tuning pegs with your picking hand.

- From there, try to tune up the remaining strings whenever you can get one of your hands free.

This is not an easy situation, and no one will expect you to recover from it fully while you're in the heat of performance… we've all been there. You probably will not be able to completely retune before the song is over, and you will need to interrupt the set for a minute while you do retune, but, thanks to your new super-tuning powers, you can get a reference pitch from someone else in the band and be ready to play before the audience even realizes that there's been a glitch.

The point is: a broken string in the middle of a performance is only a minor disaster, and certainly one that can be overcome quickly by using your ears immediately instead of having to rely on your tuner. The audience just wants to hear music, and most likely won't care if you're a few microtones out of tune!

Part 3: Altered Tunings

One of the wonderful things about the guitar is its adaptability to any playing situation. There's no law that says a guitar must always be tuned, from low to high, E A D G B E. Any or all of these strings can be tuned to any pitch a player desires!

In this section we will discuss four of the most common altered tunings: Standard Tuning Down One Half-Step, Drop D, Open D, and Open G. (CD Track 11)

A. Standard Tuning Down One Half-Step (low to high: E♭ A♭ D♭ G♭ B♭ E♭)

Some artists who have employed this tuning: Jimi Hendrix, Live, The Wallflowers, Stevie Ray Vaughan, Randy Rhoads, Alice in Chains, and Smashing Pumpkins.

This tuning is easy to play in because, like its name states, it's simply standard tuning transposed down one half-step. As stated in Part 1, some bands prefer to play in this tuning exclusively because it allows vocalists to hit higher notes a little more easily. Another advantage to this tuning is that it allows bands to play songs in uncommon keys. For example, you can use the same chord shapes and fingerings that you would to play a song in the key of E and play that same song in E♭ just by tuning down one half-step.

Track 12 on the CD provides the reference pitches for this tuning, and Track 13 is a short demonstration of how this tuning sounds. Follow along with the music below.

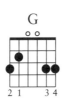

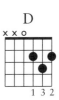

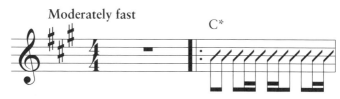

*All chords sound one half-step lower than written—actual key: A♭

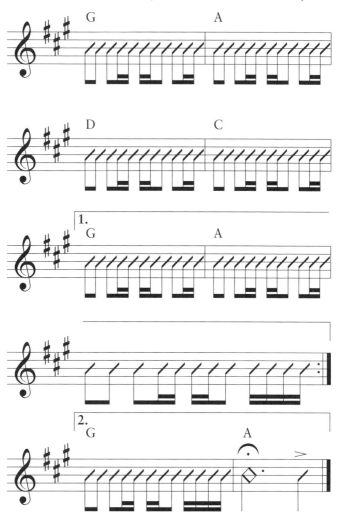

B. Drop D Tuning (low to high: D A D G B E)

Some artists who have employed this tuning: Stone Temple Pilots, Filter, Soundgarden, Rage Against the Machine, Helmet, and Tool.

This is a great tuning for hard rock because it opens up a world of power chords that can be played with only one finger. Simply by barring the three lowest strings at any given fret, you can produce rich, menacing, full-sounding chords.

Another advantage to this tuning is its extended range; specifically, the guitar (or bass) can now go as low as D, instead of E. Also, the tuning itself is extremely simple; just start in standard tuning, and as the name implies, "drop" the low E to D! You can check the new tuning by checking the 12th fret harmonic on the low E string against the open D string.

Listen to Track 14 on the audio for reference pitches for this tuning, and then listen to Track 15 for a demonstration. Again, follow along with the music below if you like.

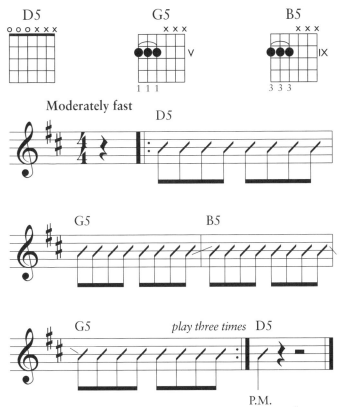

C. Open D Tuning (low to high: D A D F♯ A D)

Some artists who have employed this tuning: Joni Mitchell, countless blues/slide guitarists such as Muddy Waters, Robert Johnson, and Elmore James.

This is one of two tunings we will discuss where the open strings produce a chord. These kinds of tunings are called *open tunings*.

Early blues and slide guitarists favored open tunings because they allowed for easy slide playing over the blues form. Let's take a look at the three basic chords of a blues progression in the key of D which are D, G, and A. If a guitar is tuned to a D chord, then a G chord can be easily played by laying only one finger (or a slide) completely across all six strings at the 5th fret. Subsequently, the A chord can be played in a similar manner at the 7th fret. Refer to the following chord frames for an illustration:

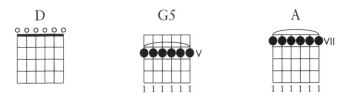

Track 16 provides reference pitches for this tuning; listen to Track 17 for a demonstration. You may also want to take note of the tablature, which shows how certain single-note, slide phrases can be played easily over the span of a fret.

D. Open G Tuning (low to high: D G D G B D)

Artists who have employed this tuning: Keith Richards, The Black Crowes, Muddy Waters, and Robert Johnson.

The advantages to this tuning are similar to those of the open D tuning.

Also worth mentioning is that this tuning is not only for slide playing. Many non-slide playing artists, such as, Keith Richards and Joni Mitchell have used open G tuning with much success. In addition, open G tuning allows for the playing of chord voicings that are not possible in standard tuning.

Listen to Track 18 for reference pitches and then to Track 19 for a demonstration.

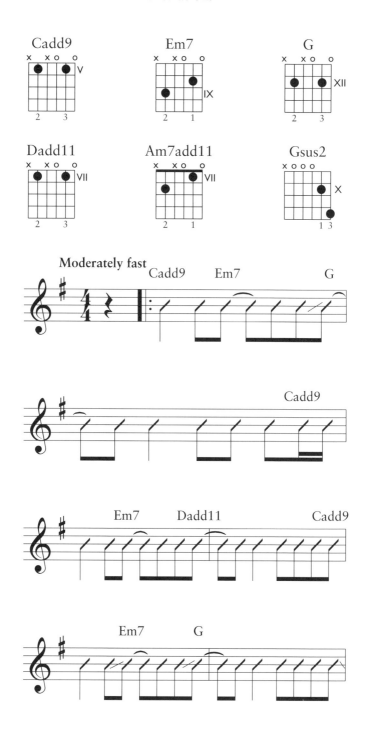

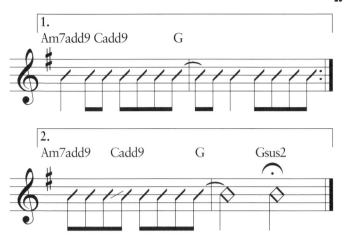

The discussion of these four altered tunings should serve as a springboard for you to try others. There's no limit to how many tunings you can use (or invent) and the new sounds which can be created as a result. Stephen Stills used a tuning of E E E E B E for the Crosby, Stills, and Nash classic "Suite: Judy Blue Eyes." The late Michael Hedges used a tuning of D A D G C D for "The Rootwitch," from the Windham Hill album Taproot. Joni Mitchell has used, off the top of my head, over seventy different tunings and has never learned to play in standard tuning. And it's not only musicians of legendary status who have discovered altered tunings... Mötley Crüe plays in standard tuning down one whole-step (D G C F A D).

The moral? Experiment! There's no wrong tuning (as long as the guitar is in tune with itself!).

Appendix: Changing Your Strings

Good news! You don't have to read this whole section—just the parts that apply to whatever type of instrument you play. Before you get into it, remember these pointers which apply to all guitar-type instruments.

- If you are changing an entire set of strings (as opposed to just replacing one), *don't tune each one up to pitch until you get all of them on*. Just tune them up enough so that they are taut and won't become unwound.

- If you are putting on an entire set of strings, don't do it sequentially. Alternate, starting with the lowest string, then the highest, then the next-lowest, and so on. This makes it easier on the neck by somewhat balancing the tension on both sides.

- Don't clip excess string length until after you've put the string on and tuned it to pitch! You'd think this would be common sense but you wouldn't believe how many "pros" forget this. I won't point any fingers, but let's just say I should take my own advice. The rule of thumb is to leave enough string at the post to wind it around three or four times.

- Most electric guitar headstocks either have all six tuning pegs on one side, like a Fender or Ibanez, or three tuning pegs on either side, as do most acoustics. Be sure to thread the strings from the inside of the tuning post, or the side opposite the tuning peg.

- *For electric guitars with whammy bars:* There are many different types of locking tremolo systems on the market today. Floyd Rose, Kahler, Steinberger, and many other manufacturers of guitars and guitar accessories produce dozens of variations on locking tremolos, non-locking tremolos, front-loading, rear-loading systems, and so on. To cover all of these would go beyond the scope of this book, so if you play a guitar with one of these systems, please refer to your guitar's owner's manual (if you bought it new) or take it to a music store to have it set up properly. For the purposes of this appendix, we'll cover the rear-loading/non-locking or "standard" tremolo system.

That's all… let's rock.

A. Steel-String Acoustic

On the bridge you'll find plastic pegs which serve to hold the strings in. They resemble fangs or long teeth, which is just as well because at times it's like pulling teeth to get them out of the bridge. You'll probably need a coin, key, or anything thin and stronger than a potato chip to help pry the peg loose.

After you get the pegs out, take a break. You deserve it.

Now take the ball end of the new string and put it in the proper hole in the bridge. Use one of the bridge pegs to push it in, aligning the grooved part with the string. After the string is in, go ahead and push the peg in completely. While pressing down on the bridge peg, tug lightly on the string to secure it against the peg.

As you thread the other end of the string through the post of the tuning peg, remember to allow enough extra string to be able to wind it around three or four times, and make sure you're threading it from the inside of the tuning post, or the side opposite the tuning peg.

When you've gotten all the strings on, perform the tune/yank/tune/yank string-settling technique mentioned on page 16 in Part 2, and you're set!

B. Nylon-String Acoustic

Nylon strings do not have ball ends, so you needn't think you bought the wrong strings when you take them out of the package!

Take the end of the new string and thread it straight through the bridge (in the direction of the bottom of the guitar). Give yourself about two inches of extra string to dangle out of the bottom of the bridge.

Take this extra length of string and bend it back towards the bridge. Now thread it under the string, wind it back around itself once or twice (I prefer twice), and pull it tight until it faces the bottom of the bridge. You may want to use a pair of needle-nose pliers to gently pull it as tightly as possible.

Now thread the other end of the string through the appropriate tuning peg. (You'll notice that the posts are horizontal.) No problem; thread the string from top to bottom (or front to back, depending on which way the post happens to be aligned).

Leave enough string length at the top to wind it around the post three or four times. When you've gotten all the strings on, gently perform the tune/yank/tune/yank string-settling technique described on page 16 of Part 2.

C. Electric, Front or Bridge-Loading, Non-Tremolo

Thread the new string through the appropriate hole at the bottom of the bridge.

As you thread the other end of the string through the post of the tuning peg, remember to allow enough extra string to be able to wind it around three or four times, and make sure you're threading it from the inside of the tuning post, or the side opposite the tuning peg.

When you've gotten all the strings on, perform the tune/yank/tune/yank string-settling technique mentioned on page 16 in Part 2, and make lots of noise.

D. Electric, Rear-Loading with Standard, Non-Locking Tremolo

Strings on these types of guitars (Fender Strats are good examples) are loaded through the back of the guitar. Once you get the strings through the bridge the rest is easy... just remember that the six holes in the back are in the opposite direction of the string order.

When you look at a guitar with the front facing you, you'll see that the left-to-right string order is low-to-high. When you turn the guitar over this order is reversed, so just keep in mind that the lowest string goes in the last (right-hand) hole, and the highest string goes in the first (left-hand) hole.

Other than that, the method for putting strings on is the same as that explained in the section on Electric, Front or Bridge-Loading, Non-Tremolo.

E. Bass

Refer to the section on *Electric, Front or Bridge-Loading, Non-Tremolo*. Different instrument, but same principle.

Further Reading

This book was designed to give you a simple, straightforward working musician's guide to tuning and overcoming tuning problems. If you have further interest in guitar maintenance, I recommend the following books.

Hedick, Brook. *Using Your Guitar.* New York: Acorn Music Press, 1980

Kamimoto, Hideo. *Electric Guitar Setups.* New York: Amsco Publications, 1994.

Kamimoto, Hideo. *Complete Guitar Repair.* New York: Oak Publications, 1978.

It is a good idea to have your guitar or bass checked for intonation problems professionally at least once. It's inexpensive, and with proper care of your instrument, it will go a long way (even years) in maintaining easy tuning.

About the Author

Matt Scharfglass is a New York-based songwriter, bassist, multi-instrumentalist, and transcriber of guitar and bass music. Hundreds of his transcriptions appear regularly in magazines such as *Guitar World* and in books published by Music Sales, Hal Leonard, and Warner Brothers. Other books he has authored for Music Sales include *Beginning Blues Bass, The Gig Bag Book of Practical Pentatonics,* and *First Step: Guitar for Kids*.

In addition to gigging around the New York City area with various artists, Matt is the leader of indie rock band Mrs. Grundy, with two releases to his credit: *Your Stinky Candy* (1999) and *Booger* (2000). You can get in touch with him at www.mrsgrundy.com.